HIDING THE SIGNS

Hiding the Signs

Copyright © 2007 Daryl Hubbard
First Edition – First Printing March 2007
Library of Congress Number pending

ISBN # 978-0-9791154-8-6

Published by Main Street Publishing, Inc., Jackson, TN.
Copy Editing by Shari B Hill
Cover Design Annette Galloway
Printed and bound by NetPub, Poughkeepsie, NY.

For more information write Main Street Publishing, Inc.,
206 East Main St., Suite 207, P.O. Box 696, Jackson, TN 38302
Phone 1-731-427-7379 or toll free 1-866-457-7379.

E-mail: words@mspbooks.com for managing editor and
mspsupport@charterinternet.com for customer service. Visit us at
www.mainstreetpublishing.com and www.mspbooks.com.

HIDING THE SIGNS

BY

DARYL K. HUBBARD

Main Street Publishing, Inc - Jackson, Tennessee

"I am black,
I am an American,
however, I am a human first."

Daryl K. Hubbard

Dedication

This book is dedicated to every young person who wants to attain a proper education.

A special dedication to my Mother, Gladys Perkins.

To my brothers, Dennis and Nate, and to all of my nieces and nephews.

Thanks to all of my friends, especially Alley Crew, and to anyone who has supported me through the years.

Special thanks to Connie Taylor and Ida Williams who helped so much with this endeavor.

HIDING THE SIGNS

Foreword

"The trouble with the younger generation is that it hasn't read the minutes of the last meeting" Man In Crisis

The original title of this book was supposed to be "You Won't Find It Here" because I wanted my young readers to go out and find the answers to the plethora of questions that I asked in the book. You see part of the problem facing many young people today is that they don't really have anything to do, hence the true purpose of this effort. Too many of our young men and women can be seen just roaming the streets like zombies wasting precious time - time that could be used enhancing their brains. And it has been said that "he who wastes time kills an eternity." I also thought about entitling this manuscript "Dumb Ain't Cute" because far too many of our young people are extremely proud to be dumb, and many behave as if they wouldn't have it any other way. It appears as if we have come to believe that being smart is weird, and that being stupid is some type of badge of honor to be proudly displayed. Many pundits and social gurus keep asking why our prisons are so full and our schools are so empty. This book, if taken seriously, will definitely reverse this terrible trend and will help place more black kids in college and less black kids in prison. It is my belief that this book will reduce America's genocidal murder rate. A murder rate so astronomical that if the major media outlets would report how many young people are maimed and murdered daily in this country, the war in Iraq would play second fiddle. This book, if read, would reduce crime, A.I.D.S., teen pregnancy, and many of the social ailments that poison us and prohibit black people from operating full scale in mainstream America. Of course, not everyone will concur with my concept, but as Gwendolyn Brooks once said, "Truth tellers are not always palatable. There is a preference for candy bars." Therefore, even after I publish this clarion call for educational achievement, informing our young people to understand that education has ceased to a privilege only to become a necessity, I know that many (okay all) of America's jails will remain open for those who scoff at this simple road map to success. In this era of navigation systems, sophisticated technology, smart bombs, and other major advances, for some strange reason the signs to prosperity and success have remarkably remained hidden from our young people. This book, even if moderately used can be an underground railroad for today's children. It can be an escape route away from the twin perils of guns and drugs, often mysteriously placed in their neighborhoods by others. We as a people should find it quite amazing that with the advent of computers, video games, television, etc., our kids still used the term <u>bored</u>. While these things may be fun, they do nothing for their brains, the body's most important muscle. And once our kids understand that brain power trumps black power, white power, or any other power, they will not only succeed in school, they will excel. This is why I'm saying it loud and clear; if we want our kids to do well in school we must encourage them to read. Every conversation that we have with our kids must begin with the Question, "What are you reading?"

I finally decided on the title "Hiding the Signs"

because in October 2006 my friends Richard Berryman, Siegfried Tharpe, and I attended my alma mater, Knoxville College's homecoming celebration. We decided to attend a function that was being held at the Women's College Basketball Hall of Fame. We received directions and proceeded to drive there. However, as we got close to our destination, the street signs were less than clear, similar to the signs that television, radio, the Internet, and major media outlets give to our young people. Our kids have been indoctrinated by the likes of C-Murder, Skinny Pimp, 50 Cent, and Flavor Flav and have been directed away from the Thurgood Marshalls, Nelson Mandelas, Eldridge Cleavers, and Cornell Wests of the world. It is no wonder that so many of our young people are in trouble and/or incarcerated because the aforementioned young men are stealing the signs; the latter group knows the routes and understands that the signs are being hidden from our kids in an almost diabolical fashion.

We need not be in the business of hiding the signs of educational enlightenment if we intend to remain a civilized society. We can no longer afford to metaphorically "eat our own" and expect to be a healthy nation capable of being a respected world power. So my message to white society is to encourage you not to be culpable in this hiding the signs conspiracy, especially those in Hollyweird and on Madison Avenue. My message to young blacks is to understand that staying lost is not only hazardous to your health but to the health of your families. There is no way a young person who has read Fanon, Baldwin, Ellison, or Wright, could be even moderately capable of committing a senseless homicide.

In effect, if we **really** are interested in stopping the drugs and murders, we must no longer hide the signs that point our young people in the right direction. We must expose those things and elements that hinder the development of our young people and guide them to the things and signs that will make life in America (the world's greatest country) wonderful for them.

HIDING THE SIGNS

"There is no difference between the man who doesn't read and the man who can't"

Hiding the Signs

Introduction

This book is my attempt to alleviate the growing ignorance permeating today's African American community, particularly amongst our young men. It may be molded or modeled to fit any grade level, including institutions of higher learning. Ralph Waldo Emerson once said, "Life is a festival only to the wise." I find it moronic, I mean ironic, that the leaders of this country have always known that having a brain provides the easiest access to heaven right here on earth, and yet they, for some strange reason, want to keep that knowledge from black children. I also find it quite troubling that white media moguls try (**and with much success**) to induce all of our young people to be like Mike, Nelly, and T.O. for example, but ignore the plethora of successful black men and women as Dr. Ben Carson, Dr. Martin Luther King, Dr. Michael Eric Dyson, Eric Dickey, and Dr. Wesley C. McClure and others, who through their intellectual prowess have changed Americas landscape. I also find it confusing that people consistently tell our children to get an education but fail to mention how to achieve this goal or provide them with an adequate road map that they can use to get to this very important destination. I feel that we cannot continue to lie, to, mislead and confuse our children by telling them to get something but not informing them what getting an education entails. This is one of the primary reasons that America has created what I term "an educational caste system."

White youth can oftentimes model appropriate educational behavior, while black children are often left to model the worlds of B.E.T. (BLACK EXTERMINATION TELEVISION), or the likes of "Pimp My Ride" "cribs" and Flavor Flav. Therefore, I am going to say this loud and clear to our children: **YOU CANNOT GET A REAL EDUCATION IF YOU DON'T DEVELOP A LOVE FOR BOOKS**. I repeat: you cannot get a real education if you don't develop a love of books. I don't care if you are a senior in high school or a senior in college; if you don't have a love for books, you are not an educated individual. It has often been said, "When a man's education is finished he is finished." I say, **"If a man doesn't develop a love for books his education never gets started."**

    In many of today's African American

communities, particularly in urban areas our kids do not even begin to get an education because they have not been taught the huge advantages that will be afforded them if they begin to voraciously consume books.

Carter G. Woodson stated in his more than famous book that **"when a Negro has finished his education in our schools, then he has been equipped to begin the life of an American or Europeanized white man."** We must understand today our public schools (**and many private schools**) are not in the business of educating our young. They are for the most part expensive and expansive advanced day care centers; and if they teach our children anything, it is how to be social zombies, fit only to work for white people, entertain white people, or to keep our burgeoning criminal justice system operating at full throttle.

It is my hope that those who take the time to read this book (**or any book for that matter**) will no longer fall prey to the ever-growing maelstrom of ignorance that has left so many of our young people dead, truncated, or incarcerated here in America, allegedly the world's greatest country. Ralph Ellison said it best when he said, **"There are few things in the world as dangerous as sleepwalkers."** This book is my attempt to wake up our young people before they are swallowed whole by their own ignorance or the ignorance of the ruling elite.

This book is an educational maze, and it is my hope that young people will put down the dope of T.V., rap music, video games (**yes, I said dope**) and follow this book through as best they can. It is also my hope that this book inspires many of our young people to start on that wonderful journey called reading - a venture that can take them to places they never imagined and away from folks with little or no imagination. Therefore, my first step would be to make sure that each and everyone has the proper materials to begin this trek, and the first essential that you will need before you begin is a library card. If you do not have a library card. STOP

"If you want to keep something from black folks, put it between the covers of a book." African-American folk saying.

Chapter I

Kweisi Mfume wrote a book titled "No Free Ride," which encourages us to always remember that nothing is free. In fact, Henry David Thoreau said, *"there is no odor so bad as that which arises from goodness tainted. It is human it is divine carrion. If I knew for a certainty that a man was coming to my house with the conscious design of doing me good, I should run for my life." If you have not read Thoreau's "On Man and Nature,"*

In his book Thoreau said, "He who wants help wants everything," which is akin to the old saying that if you give a man a fish, he eats for a day; if you teach him to fish, he may eat for a lifetime. In today's educational environment, this is tantamount to saying, "If you send a kid to school, you educate him for a day, if you teach him to love to read, you educate him for a lifetime." We as a people must understand that we cannot depend on others to educate (or miseducate) us. Our education is our own responsibility, and we forget this at our own peril.

I have to laugh (to keep from crying) every February when black folks clamor so about black history month. What a joke, and I'm sure that if Mr. Carter Woodson were alive today, he'd commit suicide if his name were even connected with such a farce. First, it is reprehensible to ask white people to celebrate a history that they don't know or care to know, and secondly, it is preposterous to only introduce this material to our children twenty-eight (28) days every year. Not only is Black history month every month, but also every day is black history day. But my people are often placated by those who offer hackneyed excerpts about black leaders of the past most notably: **Rosa Parks, Martin Luther King, and Malcolm X**. And while white television gives our kids the full view of Flavor Flav, they are limited to sound bites and hackneyed quotes from our true leaders of the past. One of our greatest leaders was **Minister El Hajh Malik El Shabazz,** who was also an autodidact. If you don't know what an autodidact is, **STOP**. **Minister Shabazz** was also known as **Malcolm X**. If you have not read the Autobiography of Malcolm X, **STOP**

The recurring theme in all of the stories of our leaders of the past is how their educational enlightenment changed not only their lives but ours as well. People like **Biko, Dubois, Mandela, Garvey, Evers,**

Bethune, all have made a positive impact on our society. If you don't know the first names of these leaders, **STOP**

When you allow others to teach you your history, you miss so much. I know many people know that Dr. Martin Luther King, Jr., won a Nobel Peace Prize. But who was **Alfred Nobel**? **STOP**

If you don't know the name of the book written by Dr. King, **STOP**

I really wish everyone who is reading this book would read the entire book, and I especially urge this for older readers. But I want each and every one of you to at least read "Chapter Five," **Letter from a Birmingham Jail**. **STOP**

In 1963, Dr. King gave a famous speech in Washington D. C. Find Dr. King's speech and read it. **STOP**

Anyone who has ever been around small black

children can see the hope and joy in their loving eyes, and yet it takes only a few years for the joy and hopes to evaporate only to be replaced with what Cornell West terms "nihilism." We must make it known that an educated man is a joyful man, and we must do, as we often did in the past before integration, instill in our young people the belief that they can do or become anything that they want to be; it just takes a little work. Read pages three (3) through six (6) of Robert Fulgum's book, **"All I Need to Know I Learned in Kindergarten."**

"The Job of the Writer is to make Revolution Irresistible" Toni Cade Bambara

Chapter II

Find and read the Bill of Rights. Amendments 1 – 19. STOP

History can often be broken down into two words his-story, and most times the winners of wars get to write their view of the story. We must learn to always view history like a coin, keeping in mind that history like a coin always has two sides.

America has been involved in numerous military conflicts in her short history. Who did America fight to gain her independence? STOP Who won the War Between the States? STOP Who won World War I? STOP Who won World War II? STOP

George W. Bush is the 43rd President of the United States. If you can't name the last seven U. S. Presidents, [STOP] Which President was nicknamed "**unconditional surrender**?" [STOP] Which President was nicknamed "Tricky Dick?" [STOP] Who was the president during Watergate? [STOP]

- John F. Kennedy was assassinated in Dallas in 1963. How many presidents have been assassinated? [STOP]

- December 7, 1941, is a day that President Roosevelt said **would live in infamy**. What happened? [STOP]

- On September 11, 2001, what major event occurred? [STOP]

HIDING THE SIGNS

- Find a copy of **<u>Roberts' Rules of Order</u>** and read Chapter 1. STOP

- Who is **Ken Hamblin?** STOP

- Who shot Bobby Kennedy? STOP

"I have never been contained except I made the prison"
Mari Evans

Chapter III

It has been said that he who reads the great classics can never be intimidated by anyone. **Franz Fanon** similarly added, **"Mastery of language affords one remarkable power."** Reading the classics not only teaches young people that their life is no where near as bad as they had imagined, but also that there are always others worse off than you. They teach students that situations are just that, situations, and that it is never too late to change them.

- Read *George Orwell's 1984.*

- Which Black author wrote a book called the *Invisible Man*?

- Many in the Black community use the term

"Uncle Tom." Read Harriet Beecher Stowe's *Uncle Tom's Cabin*. **STOP**

- Read Samuel Clemon's book, *Puddin Head Wilson*. **STOP**

- J. Baldwin, R. Wright, R. Ellison, J. Hope Franklin, F. Douglas, B. Seale. Find out the first names of these famous Black writers. **STOP**

- Who was **Aesop?** **STOP**

- Read three of "**Aesop's Fables.**" **STOP**

- Who were the **Brothers Grimm?** **STOP**

- Read at least three of their stories. **STOP**

- Who was **Anans**i? **STOP**

- Who was **Nat Turner?** **STOP**

- Find and read **Famous Black Quotations**. **STOP**

- Who was **David Walker?** **STOP**

- Who was **William Shakespeare**? STOP

- Read one of his plays. STOP

- Who wrote *A Tale of Two Cities?* STOP

- Who wrote *Death of a Salesman?* STOP

- Read *Who Moved My Cheese,* by Spencer Johnson. STOP

- Write down the **fifty (50) states**. STOP

"Where there is No Vision, the People Perish"

Chapter IV

One thing that amazes me about America's educational system (especially in our inner cities) is that we do not teach our young people the very things that they need to know. Our schools curriculum includes French, Latin, calculus, biology, chemistry, geography, etc. Neither of which prepares our children to deal with the one entity that they are more likely than not to deal with repeatedly: their local police force, many of which, because of anti-black legislation, have come to resemble the Gestapo. Because the Federal Government has gotten so humongous (i.e. Iraq, health care, the prison industrial complex, social security), it can no longer afford to give back to local municipalities.

Therefore, many of these municipalities, politically afraid to raise property taxes, are forced to use police departments as revenue enhancers, thereby making life for the poor and miserable even more poor and miserable. This is why our school systems ought to be in the business of warning our young people about the pitfalls of the criminal industrial complex, yet they choose to focus on a mundane, outdated curriculum that, for the most part, is no benefit to a child of the 21st century. Therefore, since it is someone's responsibility to explain the system to our young people, and since those in charge of educating our young won't do it, I guess that leaves the daunting task up to me.

First, wear your seatbelt. It is imperative that we teach our young people to wear their seatbelt, not only because it is the safe thing to do but also because in far too many states, the police have the right to pull you over just because you don't have on your seatbelt. And only those who work in law enforcement or the court system know how many of our young people are arrested primarily because they did not understand the full impact of the seatbelt law.

Second, you must pay your tickets in a timely manner. Far too many young African-American men are in prison just because they lost their driving privileges. A driver's license is probably the most dangerous thing a young black person can possess.

Third, turn your music down. Black people love to be seen. Therefore, we often turn our music up so loud that we become not only noticed but also obnoxious. No civilized human being wants to hear profane rap lyrics emanating from your vehicle, and so people's complaints force police officers to step up enforcement of anti-noise statutes. However, what I find even more alarming than these profane lyrics is the fact that many of our young people violate these statutes with drugs and/or alcohol in the vehicles. Talk about asking for trouble (**I told you, dumb ain't cute**).

Because I worked in the court system, I got a firsthand view of America's crime, (for example, the Negro Problem). And, I noticed that it's not drugs, alcohol, or guns that get so many of our young people incarcerated, but rather driving offenses. The state in its infinite wisdom believes that suspension of driving privileges will somehow prevent people from driving – (Again, I told you dumb ain't cute.) On top of that, some states suspend driving privileges for truancy, late child support, or lack of financial responsibility, (such as insurance). Many states today in the interest of revenue enhancement have worked to create a whole new class of career criminals, whose only crime is driving a car. I don't know about you, but I'm not terribly afraid of a person (who can drive) driving down the street whether he has a license or not. What we need to consider is taking the offending vehicle and auctioning it off. This is a far better remedy than locking people up, ruining lives, and using taxpayer dollars to house and keep them.

Many state legislators pass laws without talking to the people who tend to know and understand the system. Our current judicial system is mostly local, and because I admit I don't know much about higher courts, I will focus primarily on our local court systems. To begin, we must start with some terminology.

- What is a **Misdemeanor**? STOP
- What is a **Felony**? STOP
- What is a **Capias**? STOP

- What is an **Affiant**? STOP

- What is a **Subpoena**? STOP

- What is a **Citation**? STOP

- What is a **Mittimus**? STOP

- What is a **Defendant**? STOP

Anytime you are arrested you must go before the judge. The first time you go before the judge is called an arraignment. This is the time when the judge reads you your rights and reads the charges against you. This is one of the most crucial times in the defendant's judicial life. Many people plead guilty at arraignment, thereby helping to dispose of our overburdened court dockets. Many don't understand that even if you committed the offense, you have the right to plead not guilty and ask for a hearing. And many times because of the crowded docket, deals are struck at the hearing that you don't get if you plead guilty at arraignment. If you plead guilty, normally you are sentenced (if it is a misdemeanor), and your case is for the most part finished. If it is a felony, most courts just set your bond and give you a hearing date. If you plead not guilty at arraignment (which I feel you always should do), the judge will usually set a bond. Most people choose to use a bail bondsman, who charges you at least ten (10) percent of your bond. For example, if your bond is $5,000.00, the bondsman will charge you at least $500.00 plus his fees usually about $50.00. This money you do not recoup. This bond is the bondsman's guarantee that you will report back to court on your given court date. On your court date, you will once again be asked for your plea. If you are guilty, you may plead guilty then, and the district attorney will make you an offer. If it is a felony, you may ask for a hearing or have your case waived to the next higher court. My advice is this: if you go to court for anything other than a minor traffic infraction, you need to contact a lawyer.

If you are reading this book and find yourself in a courtroom, I admonish you to dress as if you're going to church, a wedding, or a job interview. Also, while most people don't know it, domestic violence offenses often prohibit a person from possessing a firearm forever. Not only may you never hunt or join the local police force, it is also in some instances a federal offense. Finally, everyone who goes before a judge has the right to ask for an expungement. An expungement keeps the offense off your record and allows you to have a clean criminal history. In conclusion, if you find yourself in front of a judge, always ask for an expungement!

- Who was **Thurgood Marshall**? STOP

- How many people are on the **Supreme Court**?

  STOP

- What is a **merger**? STOP

- Who is your **Mayor**? STOP

- Who is your **Governor**? STOP

- Who are the **Senators** from your state? STOP

- How many **Senators** are there? STOP

- Who was **Thomas Jafferson**? STOP

- Older kids (14 and up) read **Monster by**
  Sanyika Shakur. STOP

- All others, read Chicken Soup for the Teenage
  Soul, Volume I. STOP

"How Many a Man has detected a New Era in His Life from the Reading of a Book"

Chapter V

- Read Dr. Ben Carson's book, **"Gifted Hands."**

  STOP

- Listen to a **Gil Scott Herron** C.D. STOP

- Find and read a poem by **Langston Hughes.**

  STOP

- If you have not told someone that you **LOVE** him or her today. STOP

- Read, **The Pursuit of Happyness** by **Chris Gardner** STOP

- Young readers rent **The Pursuit of Happyness**

  STOP

- Learn something in **Spanish.** STOP

- Learn the **Manual Alphabet** (sign language).

- Read *George Orwell's* <u>Animal Farm</u>.

- Read today's **newspaper**.

- Read **Ben Franklin's** <u>Almanac</u>.

- Read <u>The Trouble I See By</u> by Vickie Wilson.

- Relax and enjoy a comic book.

"Ignorance can make you stupid"

Chapter VI

- Who was **Mozart?** STOP

- What is H_2O? STOP

- Study the **Metric System.** STOP

- Who was **Francis Bacon?** STOP

- Who was **Isaac Newton?** STOP

- Try and complete a **sudoko puzzle.** STOP

- Try and solve a **crossword puzzle.** STOP

- What is the definition of **Algebra?** STOP

- What is the definition of **Biology?** STOP

- What is the definition of **Chemistry?** STOP

- What is a **Limerick?** STOP

- What is **Mensa?** STOP

HIDING THE SIGNS

- Who was **William Faulkner**? STOP

- Who was **Daniel Fahrenheit**? STOP

- Who was **Clarence Birdseye**? STOP

- Who was **Alexander Fleming**? STOP

- Who was **Sojourner Truth**? STOP

- Who was **Marcus Garvey**? STOP

"What is the hardest task in the world? To think!

Chapter VII

- Read the book "Roots" by Alex Haley, or watch the movie. . **STOP**

- Get a **dictionary** and read through the **A's**. **STOP**

- Who was **Steven Biko**? **STOP**

- Who was **Emmitt Till**? **STOP**

- Who is **Drew T. Brown, III**? **STOP**

- Read <u>**Up from Slavery**</u> by Booker T. Washington. **STOP**

- Name one book by **Omar Tyree, Eric J. Dickey, Walter Mosley, Gary Hardwick, R.M. Johnson, E. Lynn Harris, and Tavis Smiley.** **STOP**

- Read the <u>**Coldest Winter Ever**</u> by Sister Souljah. **STOP**

45

"Those of us who refuse to read are so easily deceived."

Chapter VIII

Again, I find myself amazed by the lack of real education happening or not happening inside of our public school system. One of the most important decisions of a persons life is whether or not he or she will be religious, and yet public schools because of liberal pressure groups like the ACLU tend to shun religion altogether, thereby leaving our kids ignorant about a subject that may be the difference between choosing life or death.

- What is **Christianity**? STOP
- What is **Islam**? STOP
- What is a **Catholic**? STOP
- What is a **Mormon**? STOP

- What is a **Protestant?** STOP

- Who is the **Pope?** STOP

- Who is the head of the **Nation of Islam?** STOP

- Read at least one chapter in the **Bible.** STOP

- What is the **Koran?** STOP

- What is an **Atheist?** STOP

- What is an **Agnostic?** STOP

- Read Dan Brown's **Angels and Demons** or **The Davinci Code.** STOP

- For young readers rent **Coach Carter.** STOP

- Who was **Zeus?** STOP

- What is **Buddhism?** STOP

- What is **Hinduism?** STOP

- Who was **Confucious?** STOP

- What is **Judaism?** STOP

HIDING THE SIGNS

- Who was **Reinhold Niebuhr**?

- What is **Zionism**?

- Who is **Shelby Steele**?

"The lifetime curse of black people is the one-party system." George Will

Chapter IX

- What is a **Liberal**? [STOP]

- What is a **Conservative**? [STOP]

- What is a **Communist**? [STOP]

- What is a **Moderate**? [STOP]

- Who wrote the **Communist Manifesto**? [STOP]

- Who wrote **Black Skin, White Masks**? [STOP]

- Who wrote **Moby Dick**? [STOP]

- Who wrote **The Bluest Eye**? [STOP]

- Who wrote **Confessions of a White Racist**?

  [STOP]

- Who wrote the **Emperor of Ocean Park**? [STOP]

HIDING THE SIGNS

- Read the **<u>Emperor of Ocean Park</u>"** 🛑

- A. J. Jacobs wrote **<u>The Know-It-All</u>**, Read A

  through D. 🛑

"The Negro pays for what he wants and begs for what he needs." Kelly Miller

Chapter X

Today in the African-American community, you see many instances of financial infancy. We bling, bling, buy expensive cars, clothes, etc. We technically just live for today. All of our movies and music focus on conspicuous consumption and everywhere you visit stores in the African-American communities are owned by others. Is our self-hate such that we won't even support each other economically? Chancellor Williams said in his book *"The Destruction of Black Civilization."* If we say that, as a race, we are too poor to engage in productive activities that would create thousands of jobs for our young people-if we continue "traditional" pleas of poverty, our total spending of 40 to 42 billion dollars each year rises up to call us liars."

- Read "Financial Peace" by Dave Ramsey. **STOP**

We must learn to respect our financial power much more than we do today. If we become patient with our money, the loan sharks, rent to own, and check cashing institutions that permeate poor communities would go out of business almost instantly. We must understand that if we want something, buying it with cash is our only salvation. Dave Ramsey is an economic genius and if we have any hopes of ridding ourselves of these economic parasites, we must part with our old ways of doing business. Credit is a bad word; and if we want to stop being economic and therefore political slaves, we must change our counter productive consumption habits. "**Because it is only the fool whose own tomatoes are sold to him**."

- Read <u>The Invisible Man</u> by Ralph Ellison.

  STOP

- Watch <u>Eyes on the Prize</u>. STOP

- Browse the book *100 Amazing Facts About the Negro with Complete Proof* by J. A. Rogers. STOP

- Read <u>Forty Acres</u> by Phyllis Dixon.

<u>The End</u>

HIDING THE SIGNS

Selected Reading

- *The Bible*
- *The Pearl by John Steinbeck*
- *Soul on Ice by Eldridge Cleaver*
- *Native Son by Richard Wright*
- *The Souls of Black Folk by W.E.B. Dubois*
- *Chicken Soup for the Soul by Jack Canfield*
- *The Second American Revolution by Gore Vidal*
- *Devil In a Blue Dress by Walter Mosley*
- *The Communist Manifesto by Karl Max and Frederick Engles*
- *The Wretched of the Earth by Fratz Fanon*
- *Zen and the Art of Motorcycle Maintenance by Robert Pirsing*
- *Hamlet by William Shakespeare*

- *Babbitt by Sinclair Lewis*
- *Pick a Better Country by Ken Hamblin*
- *The Way Things Ought to Be by Rush Limbaugh*
- *Dionetics by L. Ron Hubbard*
- *Sweet St. Louis by Omar Tyree*
- *Race Matters by Cornell West*
- *The Choice by Samuel Yette*
- *Makes Me Wanna Holler by Nathan McCall*
- *The Three Musketeers by Alexander Dumas*
- *The Price of the Ticket by James Baldwin*
- *The Coming Crisis of Western Sociology by Alvin Gouldner*
- *Walden by Henry David Thoreau*
- *Dreams From My Father - Barack Obama*
- *Biko by Donald Woods*
- *Black Skin, White Masses by Frantz Fanon*

- *1001 Things Everyone Should Know About American History by John A. Garraty*
- *Black Like Me by John Howard Griffin*
- *The West and the Rest of Us by Chinweizu*
- *Religions of the World Made Simple by John Lewis*
- *The Coming Oil War by Doug Clark*
- *Blind Ambition by John Dean*
- *Oedipus the King by Sophocles*
- *An The Walls Came Tumbling Down by Ralph Abernathy*
- *Mythology by Edith Hamilton*

HIDING THE SIGNS

Biography

Daryl Hubbard is a former columnist with the Jackson Sun in Jackson, Tennessee. Currently an elected official in Jackson, Daryl started working as Jackson City Court Clerk in August 1998. He has more that twenty-five years experience working with young people and has enjoyed a first hand view of America's education system. Daryl is a graduate of Knoxville College in Knoxville, Tennessee and attended Graduate school at the University of Memphis. He father of two children, Daryl and Dominique. Daryl and his two brothers were raised in Detroit, Michigan and attended the Detroit public schools.

Main Street Publishing, Inc.
206 E. Main Street Suite 207
P.O.Box 696
Jackson, Tn 38301

Toll Free #: 866-457-7379
or
Local #: 731-427-7379

Visit us on the web:
www.mainstreetpublishing.com
www.mspbooks.com

E-Mail: mspsupport@charterinternet.com